About Dr. MacLeod

Greg MacLeod is a philosopher, social activist, entrepreneur and Catholic priest. In 1973 he co-founded New Dawn Enterprises, which has grown into a multimillion-dollar business employing more than 150 people in his native Cape Breton, Nova Scotia. Dr. MacLeod is also Professor Emeritus at Cape Breton University, a member of the Order of Canada and the recipient of numerous honourary degrees. His previous books include: *From Mondragon to America: Experiments in Community Economic Development* and *New Age Business: Community Corporations that Work.*

© Greg MacLeod, Ph.D.
Director
Tompkins Institute
Cape Breton University

Published 2010, Tompkins Institute
ISBN: 978-0-9732682-2-5

Editing and design by

Write Away
Design & Editing
write_away@soon.com

Contents

Seven Steps

Because I have been involved in organizing community-based businesses for almost 40 years, many people have asked me to write a "how to" guide. Often the requests come from academics deeply concerned about social or economic disparity, while others come from activists anxious to get their communities more involved in solving inequality.

As an academic philosopher accustomed to teaching first-year students, I have learned to keep things simple. An effective method is to provide numerous paths to a few central ideas, allowing each person to choose his or her own. So, this guide is divided into seven simple steps that follow real-life examples to arrive at conclusions.

The steps are followed by two chapters that examine the environment in which we work. The first identifies the components of local infrastructure that appear to be a prerequisite for successful business development (because economically distressed communities often lack this infrastructure we need to build it ourselves). The second focuses on the mechanistic economic models that are ushering in the era of mega-cities without, in my opinion, considering the effects this is having on ecology and smaller communities.

Keep in mind that I am writing from personal experience and observation. I have often been shocked by arm-chair activists who write detailed books on how to set up projects even though they have never done so themselves and offer no practical advice from those who have. Beware of those who insist: "This is the way it should be done." Always ask: "How do you know?" A dose of what philosophers label empiricism, and what most people call practical experience, always comes in handy.

Greg MacLeod
Sydney, Cape Breton
December 2009

1   Start a small group of three or four activists.

2   Agree on your purpose and strategy.

3   Examine existing community businesses and form alliances where possible.

4   Identify a few business opportunities.

5   Find financial and human resources.

6   Establish a flexible legal structure that allows growth.

7   Launch your business cautiously, but without great delay.

A Handful of Activists

This guide is for those who are concerned about the lack of economic well-being and vitality in their communities and are ready to do something about it. Instead of waiting for outside authorities to take the initiative, there are concrete things you can do now. I assume that you are an academic, a trade unionist, an activist in the cooperative movement, a member of a chamber of commerce or a church group concerned about social justice, or someone who simply wants to make a difference.

In any of these groups, there will be at least two people who are concerned enough to do something. I say two because any social movement requires more than one person.

Many young people have come to me brimming with enthusiasm to start a community organization. They overflow with ideas and energy. This is not enough. Usually, I tell them to convince a few of their friends to join them. That's the tricky part; often they cannot.

The hardest stage in building an organization is finding at least one other person who shares your purpose or attitude. Once you have found that person, you must talk a lot to determine whether or not you agree on a problem that needs to be solved. The problem could be unemployment in your area. It could be the lack of affordable housing or the high cost of food for low-income people. If you agree that there is a problem, then you must decide whether you want to try to solve it.

> Many young people have come to me brimming with enthusiasm to start a community organization. They overflow with ideas and energy. This is not enough.

➲ Recruiting

Some will look for recruits who have the right political attitude. Some will seek out left-leaning people and

> It is a common mistake to organize a community-business team on the basis of moral commitment without regard to skills.

shun business people. I find, however, that a lot of very good people don't categorize themselves. Many would not even know how to define "socialist" or "capitalist."

So, I suggest two much more important characteristics to look for. One is at the moral level: it is a spirit of generosity and a personal commitment to help improve the local community. The second is at the level of action: does the person have the right skills to contribute to the development of a successful business?

Some people have great personal commitment, but they are much better at talking than doing. This is not a matter of faults or qualities. Some people seem born with the ability to sing. Others are tone deaf and will never learn to carry a tune.

All of us have different kinds of contributions to make. It is a common mistake to organize a community-business team on the basis of moral commitment without regard to skills.

At the recruitment stage there are several options. Some will take the populist route. They will reason that it is a community problem and therefore they must get the community involved. They will attempt to have community meetings to recruit volunteers to help solve the problems identified. I have not seen much success in this approach, which is sometimes called "grass roots."

Communities are made up of a great variety of people: trades people, professionals, the unemployed, those on welfare, students, etc. It seems to me extremely difficult to throw out a net and expect to recruit a coherent and unified group ready for action.

➲ Advocacy or business?

I make a clear distinction between a community-advocacy organization and a community-business organization. For advocacy, broad community support is

> The unity required for advocacy is different than the unity required for business.

required. There is power in numbers. Diversity is useful because it brings inclusiveness. An advocacy group must exert enough power to change a political reality. In contrast, a business organization must create a business.

The unity required for advocacy is different than the unity required for business. An advocacy group wants to influence how another power group makes decisions, but it is not accountable for those decisions. A business group makes its own decisions and is accountable for them. In business, accountability is very concrete: usually making or losing money. It is more serious when the group is using other people's money.

➲ Volunteer leaders

Transformation of society can only take place through organization. Fundamental to the process of organizing is the role of the volunteer.

> The volunteer who works out of obligation, or even guilt, is usually not a very effective one.

The volunteer leader is an essential element in any movement to bring about social or economic change.

The vast majority of people work because they have to. They need an income to live and must work to get it. Most of the time people do gainful work not so much because they like to, but because it is the best that they can find. Work has the aspect of obligation: tasks are imposed from the outside through necessity. Leisure is activity we choose because we like it.

Volunteering is a type of leisure activity. We do it freely, because we want to. The volunteer who works out of obligation, or even guilt, is usually not a very effective one. Some people in society are fortunate in that they end up with a job that they really enjoy; they would do it even if they were not paid. For them the line between volunteer and obligatory work is blurred.

The focus here is the challenge of recruiting a few other volunteer leaders. Our special interest is social or economic change, but the techniques and principles can apply to any field that depends upon volunteer leadership. Most of the successful efforts I have seen depended upon a small nucleus of committed volunteers who were united, not simply by conviction, but also by friendship. (The mustard seed that grows into a tree.)

Friendship presupposes a basic sharing of values and attitudes. A person who is not interested in the welfare of the unemployed will not be compelled to expend a lot of energy in job creation, while those not sensitive to the plight of slum dwellers will not have great passion for building affordable housing.

My comments here are directed especially to the lead-organizer, and there has to be one. People simply don't pop up as volunteers spontaneously. A notice in a newspaper is not sufficient. First of all, most individuals must be invited or called upon to participate in an activity. There is nothing wrong with asking a friend to start a project with you.

Volunteer projects will always require a central team that is very committed and active. Social change usually starts with one or two committed people who seek out others.

In community-business projects, I have found that the effective number seems to be three or four as a nucleus. The recruitment and formation of the team is critical. I have had the experience of recruiting a team through nomination. I asked a housing organization to name a delegate, a labour council to name a delegate, etc. When I had the group together I found that the members of the team did not like each other.

One might say that they should like each other, but usually that is beyond the control of the organizer. That particular project did not succeed, simply because the lead team could not work together effectively. Meetings became a chore. The members came not because they liked to attend or because they liked the activity; they attended out of obligation.

Two of the most successful community businesses I have studied are the Mondragon Cooperative Corporation and the Valencia cooperative. In each, the basic organization was created by five friends.

I remember a meeting in Europe between a Christian and a Communist social activist who were active in Africa. In discussions about motivation, the Christian and the Communist gave two very different answers. The Christian said he was in Africa working with the poor for the love of God. The Communist said he was in Africa for the love of Africans. The two attitudes are certainly not contradictory, but one suggests obligation and sacrifice imposed from outside, while the other suggests freely chosen involvement out of a concern that is internally driven. Of course, the Christian I refer to had a distorted theology. The authentic Christian, like any authentic social activist, will help others simply because that is the humane thing to do, and because it is rewarding in itself.

➲ Friendship is vital

The first bit of advice I suggest is that the organizer begins by recruiting someone he or she likes, preferably a friend. Then the two should seek out a few others jointly, or simply ask the friend to find another person who would fit in. This does sound exclusive, but it seems to work quite well.

> The personal approach trumps a technological or ideological one.

As noted above, volunteers have free choice. They are not being paid to work, so it is difficult to expect the kind of heroic virtue that will prompt a person to voluntarily spend time with people he or she is not compatible with. Personally, I have found that people who work in the volunteer sector in an authentic way usually develop life-long relationships that are precious and mutually supportive. They make sacrifices, but gain friends.

Working in a community business can be very difficult and frustrating. It really helps when the volunteer members have an automatic understanding about the feelings of the other members. A shared sense of humour is also extremely valuable. These are the assets that are found in friendship.

Explanations are not always required; they are implicit in the relationship. (Even philosophers, who spend so much time in thought, consider friendship to be a key virtue.)

There are many, many potential volunteers in every community. They just need to be invited. That's how hockey or baseball teams are formed. The big leagues have "scouts" who seek out the best players. Again, I repeat that the invitation cannot be simply in a letter or a note in a newspaper. The invitation must be personal.

The organizer must take the time to get to know a potential recruit to determine whether or not they have shared values. The person recruited is also affirmed by the fact that an organizer takes the time to meet and discuss a project on a personal level. The personal approach trumps a technological or ideological one.

⟳ Set modest goals

Another important caution: do not ask people to do the impossible. If we wish to have a successful organization, we must always invite

> It is much better to begin with small tasks at the local level before moving on to the universal.

people to do what is doable. If we invite someone to work with us to solve climate change or lower the unemployment rate, we will often find his or her eyes will glaze over. However, if we ask for help building a couple of new houses or cleaning up a polluted stream, people will usually grasp what this entails. They will see a particular project with a beginning and an end.

Keep in mind the adage "learn by doing." As people perform simple tasks that help make the world better, they soon go on to other, bigger tasks. At the same time, they begin to understand bigger issues. It is much better to begin with small tasks at the local level before moving on to the universal.

Another key is that the lead-organizer must really believe that most people have good hearts and would want to serve their neighbours if they knew how. Hope and optimism are fundamental for successful organization. Pessimists and complainers are not pleasant people to work with.

⊃ Business skills

Once we have three or four people who want to do something about a specific problem that can be addressed using a business approach, we have made a very

> I have found it interesting that successful business people are usually not highly specialized.

good start. At this point they don't have to know how they are going to do it. The main thing is that they must have some personal commitment and some social concern. If we are dealing with academics or people from movements such as the cooperatives or trade unions, we can speak in general terms. However, most people with a moral concern about society are quite unclear about what should be done.

In organizing a job-creation project, I approached successful business people with the simple question: "You are successful in business, yet there are many unemployed people in the community. Do you think we can create some jobs for them?" A typical answer was: "The community has been good to me, I'd like to give something back. I'll do what I can."

When I was a young student, I assumed that most business people were only out for themselves. Later in life, I learned that some business people were generous and some were selfish. Also, I found that some people in the cooperative movement were generous and some were selfish. No one group has a monopoly on the virtues required for successful community business.

You may wonder what skills should be sought in the original team of volunteers. In general, I do not think that specialists are necessary. I think it is important to have one or two successful business people. I have found it interesting that successful business people are usually not highly specialized. A business person who is successful in a machine industry is usually competent to serve on the board of a housing business.

There is a set of basic business skills that any successful business person has. Sometimes it is simply "horse sense" or intuition about what makes a business work. Of course, the typical organizing team will contain a mixture of people from various backgrounds. However, if a person is opposed to all business people for ideological reasons, he or she is not going to fit in.

The simplest approach is the "crystallizing process." In the formation of crystals, two cells form two more, and they in turn form two more, and so on. Once two reach agreement, they should be the key people to pick others to join them. This is not contradictory to the cooperative principle of "open membership." This is an organizing process. Once the structures are launched and operational, then there will be new systems of selection and admittance, such as people buying shares and electing boards.

➲ Start with where you are

Enthusiasm can be dangerous, inclining us to seek the impossible. Our modest approach is inspired by a report from a group of social activists in Latin America who met in Brazil in 2000 to discuss the challenge of social economic change.

> There are important steps that local citizens can take to aid the economic reconstruction of their own society.

In that part of the world, we have seen terrible dictatorships along with shameful oppression and injustice by international companies. This history is well known. The social activists I refer to were among those anxious to change the international system and wrest control away from the multinationals that abetted the dictators. They had been fighting for 20 to 30 years. Finally, they had to admit that they had not made progress; control by the multinationals was increasing.

In the midst of this realization they came to the conclusion that the only asset they had was hope, and that meant that they had to do something. Since the global system was so powerful, they decided they would concentrate on their own backyard. Instead of attacking the international system, they decided to start at the local level. They looked around for possible development projects. I agree with this point of view.

Prominent academics now speak of "place-based" development. It is the same idea: we must start with where we are. Of course, this is not in opposition to those who seek change on a more universal level. It is simply a different starting point.

Although I am not proposing a formula or solution for the total ills of society, there are important steps that local citizens can take to aid the economic reconstruction of their own society. Since commercial enterprises are an essential part of the local system, the most sensible start concerned citizens can take is to become involved in a new way of creating local business enterprises.

All communities contain people who are generous with their time and committed to improving their societies. Normally such people work through church structures, service clubs and a wide variety of charitable organizations. This same kind of energy and commitment can be harnessed to animate the local economy.

The Consensus

Let's say the group has decided to create jobs in the local community. The problem to be tackled could just as easily be affordable housing or jobs for immigrants, but what is vital is that the group begins with a problem and not simply a cause.

Groups usually do not function well unless they first develop a shared vision. This means members must talk among themselves. Formal meetings are not required: the discussions can take place casually.

Shared vision does not mean agreement on a detailed ideology or a political platform. In the context of setting up a community enterprise, shared vision refers to a set of values. At this point, the group must be careful not to get lost in language. Discussion about values can often produce a great deal of jargon and rhetoric.

It is better to be concrete. A pragmatic way of understanding "values" is to define them as ideas you are committed to that motivate you to act in a particular way. From this perspective, we can determine what people's values are by observing how they act in their daily lives. If an idea is not somehow manifested in action then it is not a value.

The basic values of various groups may be the same, but the order of their importance and the way they are formulated will change according to historical and cultural circumstances. For instance, in the 18th century, democracy was a priority in discussion of values. However, today it is taken for granted as a value everyone agrees on. I have never heard of a political leader saying that he or she opposed democracy. Belief in democracy can be assumed.

> We can determine what people's values are by observing how they act in their daily lives. If an idea is not somehow manifested in action then it is not a value.

⊃ Shared vision

It is extremely important for those involved in social-economic movements to ensure that they share the same ideas and vision through a process of discussion, which can

> The best approach is to regard the business organization as an opportunity to learn.

bring about a reconsideration of members' ideas. Without shared significant ideas there will be no shared significant action. Based on a great deal of discussion with a wide spectrum of people involved in community-oriented business, it appears to me that five basic values seem to drive them:

1. **Money is a tool.** It ought to serve human development and not vice versa. A community business is a means of human and community development, not an end in itself.
2. **Personal commitment is required.** This is reflected in volunteer participation motivated by personal belief and not simply by personal financial reward.
3. **Democracy must be active.** It presumes that each person has one vote regardless of the amount of money put in. However, this value refers to more than the ballot. It is more of an ongoing process: a search for methods to permit participation and consultation.
4. **Management must be disciplined and competent.** This is reflected in the formation of the board and the selection of staff.
5. **The relationship with the local community is one of solidarity.** This implies personal investment to initiate more job-creating enterprises when unemployment exists.

There are many formulations of principles for the organization of community businesses. Several examples can be found in the Appendix.

In looking at a wide variety of community businesses, there appears to be a general agreement on a set of basic values even though these are not clearly expressed. However, there is no clear agreement that one or another structure is best. Indeed, most groups seem to adopt an experimental attitude, which is quite healthy. The best approach is to regard the organization as a learning opportunity; remaining open to evolution increases its chance of survival.

People are not accustomed to talking about values, so such discussions have to be somewhat indirect. In organizing BCA Holdings, I had some interesting experiences regarding values. BCA began as a small committee in New Dawn Enterprises.

New Dawn was often blocked by a lack of investment capital. It had established plenty of projects that were clearly good for the community – such as a residence for the aged, dental clinics and affordable housing – yet it could not access capital for new projects.

Eventually a committee was set up to develop an investment company. Membership in the committee changed. Members kept seeing legal and financial complications. Finally, there were three of us left on the committee. We decided to stop talking and do something. Each of us agreed to lend the new company, BCA, $5,000. We launched it with total assets of $15,000.

⮑ The money question

The agreement to invest our own money was real proof of a consensus among us. We agreed that it made sense to raise money in the local community to invest in local business development. Money can be a great test of commitment.

> What is fascinating about fund-raising is the different ways men and women react when asked to invest.

The way people react to money can be very interesting. What is fascinating about fund-raising is the different ways men and women react when asked to invest. My view may not be scientific, but it is based on experience.

A few days after launching BCA, I ran into a prominent lawyer. I told him that we had set up a not-for-profit company to raise money to develop local business and to create jobs. I asked him to invest. He replied, "What's the return?" I explained that he would be helping the community and would be paid 4 percent interest. He was not interested, saying he could get a higher return on the stock market. That was one kind of response. Others said they could afford to invest a few thousand since we were paying the market rate.

17

In contrast, the first question from women usually would be, "What are you going to do with the money?" When I explained that we needed money to lend to a community group in Reserve Mines so it could construct a building as part of its community-renewal effort, they would often say, "That sounds like a really good project. Count me in."

It turned out that most of our support came from the clergy and religious congregations. That is natural since their rationale is service and helping others. Nevertheless, we insisted on presenting ourselves as a business. I have seen that helping one's neighbour and running a successful business can be very compatible.

Consensus has to involve a commitment to action. The group must clearly agree that they will set up some kind of business that will help the community. They don't have to be clear as to how they will do it. In fact, it is better to be cautious. I like the swimmer's habit of sticking a toe into the water to test the temperature before plunging in.

Take a Look Around

Now it's time to look around. Before your group starts acting, examine what other like-minded groups are doing. In what areas have they failed and in which have they succeeded? What worked well and what didn't?

The essential question in the case of a failed project is: were the causes internal or external? If they were internal, then determine whether the failure was the result of structure or personnel. This is vital because we can control and remedy internal factors, but external ones are often beyond our control. Rare is the group that will admit it has made a mistake, but such self-appraisal is necessary for survival.

Identifying the causes of failure or success can be murky. However, there is a simple distinction that has been extremely useful to me. It is the difference between a cause that is not sufficient to make something happen (one that is not enough in itself) and one that is necessary. Besides being useful, this distinction is really quite simple. For instance, money is necessary for the development of a business, but it is not sufficient if the manager is not skillful. Likewise, a skillful manager is necessary but not sufficient if he or she has no operating cash.

As we examine examples of community business, we shall see that the cause of failure or success varies. It is never one simple factor.

Before getting involved in the organization of New Dawn, I watched many cooperative businesses being formed in Atlantic Canada. Some succeeded and some failed. One of the most successful was set up by coal miners along the lines of the British co-op tradition.

> Rare is the group that will admit it has made a mistake, but such self-appraisal is necessary for survival. Identifying the causes of failure or success can be murky.

➲ British Canadian

British Canadian Cooperative was established in 1900 by coal miners in the town of Sydney Mines who had connections with the cooperative

> The organization followed a dying board and dying management into the graveyard.

movement in Scotland. The need for this cooperative was real. The miners were poorly paid and continually in debt to the "company store." Their cooperative was a marvelous success.

Up until the 1950s, British Canadian Cooperative was the most economically impressive community-owned business in Atlantic Canada. By 1955 annual sales exceeded $3 million. Its integrated system consisted of eight branch stores throughout industrial Cape Breton, a bakery, a dairy and a member-savings program. Many of us had personal savings books adorned with the phrase, "Teach your dollars to have cents."

British Canadian, however, never became an integral part of the new co-op system being organized from Saint Francis Xavier University in Antigonish, perhaps because of religious differences. It seems that it expired mainly as a result of a lack of new leadership. Although faithful and dedicated, its board became old and entrenched. They did not join the new co-op movement and simply could not adapt to a changing commercial world. The problem of failure was not external. The idea was right, but the organization followed a dying board and dying management into the graveyard.

➲ United Maritime

Another example New Dawn looked at was United Maritime Fishermen's Cooperative (UMF). Through the efforts of Dr. Moses Coady a string

> Growth, and the economies of scale this is based on, could not be achieved in a decentralized business system.

of fishery co-ops was formed in the Atlantic area with a grant from the federal government, after the Royal Commission on Fisheries in 1927. Eventually, they formed a second-level co-op called UMF. In the mid-1980s, however, it failed.

For quite some time UMF had been suffering from a chronic lack of capital, as its members were inclined to distribute their dividends rather than build up a capital reserve. Each fishermen's co-op was autonomous and its board decided what to do with surpluses. Since co-op members were poor, the board could not resist the temptation to distribute surpluses in the form of dividends. The result, however, was that UMF was usually left vulnerable with little flexibility and an inability to survive one or two misfortunes. Healthy companies usually have an equity base that allows some risk-taking and even mistakes. UMF was never healthy in that way.

The structure of UMF was an internal problem. Economies of scale and highly qualified management can only be achieved through a level of centralization. British Canadian thrived through centralized management and control of capital. UMF, however, could not grow as long as its management and capital were decentralized.

After the establishment of New Dawn, I learned about the Mondragon model. What was fascinating to me was that this model also involved the diversification and clustering of business. Conversely, in our local experience – based on the Coady and Saint Francis Xavier initiatives – each co-op had its own board and general manager. Besides credit unions, cooperatives in Atlantic Canada have achieved very little success. After examining numerous local experiences of failure, it became obvious that growth, and the economies of scale this is based on, could not be achieved in a decentralized business system.

⊃ CBL Dev Co

Another potential base for community business is the labour movement. In 1987, I was approached by leaders of Local 1115 of the International Labourers' Union. They were deeply concerned about the high level of unemployment among their 700 members. Because of continuing high unemployment in Cape Breton, members were in debt and some were losing their homes and cars to finance companies.

> The labour movement can be a tremendous resource for alternative community businesses.

We analyzed the situation in collaboration with a resource group at Cape Breton University. The most severe problem was that some workers could not afford decent housing. We concluded, however, that if they were properly organized they would be able to build their own houses. We formed a not-for-profit company called Cape Breton Labourers' Development Corporation (CBL Dev Co), which received administrative support from the local university's Tompkins Institute during its first years.

Union members agreed to lend the company a small portion of their wages, 25 cents per hour, on an interest-free basis when they were working. You will be surprised how that added up. When about 700 workers put up 25 cents per hour, the total neared $350,000 per year, and it was interest free. For each worker it meant $10 per week, or about $500 per year. If we had asked for $500 per year some members might have been shocked, but nobody objected to 25 cents per hour.

CBL Dev Co used these funds to provide interest-free mortgages for the new homes it built. It provided construction jobs for union members as well as new homes on a lease-purchase basis. (The average payment was $300 per month for a 1,000 square foot home.)

This union-based company was an excellent example of partnership. Besides profiting from its alliance with university staff, CBL Dev Co was able to benefit from an interest-free loan from the international union office, loans from local church groups, and then matching interest-free loans from both provincial and federal governmental agencies.

The idea was to use the mortgage fund to build houses, and as the tenant-purchaser made payments on the new home the fund would be replenished and the money used to build more homes. The workers regarded their loan of 25 cents per hour as savings, which they received upon retirement.

The lesson here is that the labour movement can be a tremendous resource for alternative community businesses. By 2000, however, CBL Dev Co had begun to falter after its key leader died. Between 1987 and 2000, it had built 25 homes. However, after 2000, it ceased to build, although it still owned houses and administered the mortgages.

In retrospect the major problem was internal. I tried to convince the group to join the New Dawn system to benefit from its managerial staff. However, its members feared losing autonomy. They were very concerned about autonomy.

⮕ The autonomy fixation

"Autonomy" is one of the most common values claimed by failed community businesses. Very often a small board is elected by a small community group. Soon they reach their limits

> The other common value cited by failed community businesses is "tradition."

in business capacity and are unable to grow. Yet, they will often refuse to federate with larger groups because they fear losing autonomy. This mindset has caused many failures.

The other common value cited by failed community businesses is "tradition." When innovation is suggested some tend to resist, saying: "We have always done it this way." Doing things differently is considered a betrayal, regardless of the merits.

Successful credit unions in Canada have learned a crucial lesson: it is difficult for orphan businesses to survive. Individual credit unions often failed. However, when they learned to establish provincial centres they became much stronger. Small credit unions were able to take advantage of the expertise provided by the centres.

The best example of "strength in unity" is the Mondragon Cooperative Corporation. Founder Don Jose Maria called it an experiment. Mondragon functions on the idea that it must constantly adapt and innovate.

⮕ SIMA

In 1990, a number of Acadian co-ops in Caraquet, New Brunswick, decided to play a more active role in the struggle against unemployment. A series of meetings and

> Risk analysis is critical and this ability takes years to develop.

discussions were held among the major co-ops in the area, led by their well-

23

known leaders. The result was a new venture company comprising the six following partners:

> The Acadian Credit Unions of New Brunswick
> The Acadian Cooperative Stores of New Brunswick
> The Acadian Credit Union Insurance Company
> Co-op Atlantic
> The Federal Government
> The Provincial Government

The new organization was incorporated in December 1990 as La Societé d'Investissement du Mouvement Acadien (SIMA). The provincial government provided a $1 million interest-free loan for seven years. Another $1.6 million was provided by various co-ops and credit unions, pushing the asset base to $2.6 million by the end of 1992.

SIMA's objective was to finance local business development and job creation. Some of the clients were co-ops and some were individual and privately owned businesses. What was most important was that they were all locally owned and controlled, and the jobs and profits stayed in the local area. SIMA was a clear manifestation of the intention of co-op leaders in this region to take a leading role in solving local economic problems.

By December of 1992, SIMA had invested $357,000 in five companies, mainly in the form of share capital. The clients were a printing business, a maple sugar co-op, a funeral co-op, a natural food co-op, and a blueberry-packing plant. Besides providing capital, SIMA also provided advice and technical assistance to client companies. Client companies also had to be willing to allow SIMA delegates to sit on their boards.

After a few years, and after much frustrating effort by dedicated co-op leaders, the project failed. While any venture capital company would face difficulty in such a poor economy, SIMA seemed to have a basic internal fault. Management was not experienced and skilled in making commercial loans.

Making commercial loans is completely different from making the personal loans that are typically made by Atlantic Canadian credit unions. While SIMA's structure and financial resources were excellent, its board and management lacked the specialized kind of thinking and analysis required for commercial investment. Risk analysis is critical and this ability takes years to develop.

⊃ Mondragon

The Mondragon complex is a system of tiers with many inter-relationships. Under the Congress, its corporate umbrella, there are the three divisions: finance, distribution and industrial. Mondragon University is part of the umbrella structure with the enterprises naming one-third of the board. More than 100 industrial co-ops are involved.

> Another lesson from Mondragon is that first-rate technology creates more jobs in the long run.

In a technical sense, each is autonomous. Yet, most of these enterprises would not be able to survive if they operated outside the mutually supporting system, which includes research centres and financial institutions.

With over US$15 billion in sales a year and affiliates in more than fifteen countries, no one can challenge the fact that Mondragon is a commercial success. The key lessons from this worker-owned cooperative are:

> - It is worthwhile for community businesses to sacrifice autonomy for the sake of commercial strength. Participation in a cluster of some sort provides support.
> - It is essential for community-business development to have the support of a related financial institution.
> - Formation of staff is essential. It is not sufficient to have moral commitment; the technical ability of managers is a fundamental requirement.
> - Research is necessary for any business that aims to grow. Business in 1930 was quite simple. In the 21st century it is far more complex.
> - Effort must be made to find competent managers.

Another lesson from Mondragon is that first-rate technology creates more jobs in the long run, even though it is less labour intensive. Mondragon is proof of that. Outdated technology lowers productivity and usually leads to failure. There are many examples of community businesses in all countries. These are some of the ones I know quite well. The point is that you should take time to look at many examples before you try to start a business in and for the sake of your community.

There is quite a bit of information about these cases, much of it online. However, I advise that you visit community enterprises in your area and speak with the people involved in them. The most effective learning usually takes place face to face. In this case, discussions with people who have demonstrated an ability to help revitalize local communities are often inspiring as well as instructive.

Selecting a Business

The real test of a group's commitment is action. When the members decide to actually start a project, an extremely important distinction must be made: will they begin by forming a structure or identifying a business?

Many socially committed people are inclined to begin at the level of ideas. They wish to form co-ops or not-for-profit organizations. At one time, I would automatically have begun with theories of organization. For one thing, it is a lot simpler for a socially minded person. However, over the years, I have found it is more effective to begin with the business and leave discussions of the appropriate structure to later.

In 1970, I organized a discussion group with friends who were deeply concerned about economic decline in Cape Breton. Our backgrounds were in social activism and academia. We talked and talked and talked. We were in fundamental agreement about what was wrong, but we could not come to any consensus except that the government and "corporate welfare bums" were bad. After meetings that went on for about a year, I got tired of discussion and decided to find people who were more action-inclined. I recruited the engineer-manager of a ship repair company who lived in my neighbourhood, a real-estate salesman, and the brother of a good friend. Another recruit was a housewife.

Since housing was a problem, I asked them to help provide affordable housing. We formed the Cape Breton Association for Cooperative Housing. It happened that I had organized a school for handcrafts the year before and we had no premises, so I proposed to the group that we buy a building to house the school. It was a very concrete, simple task.

> After meetings that went on for about a year, I got tired of discussion and decided to find people who were more action-inclined.

27

⊃ Other people's money

When an abandoned commercial building became available, we analyzed the market situation and agreed that the building was

> A community group's chances of success are higher when its organizers put up their own money and participate in risk.

a good deal. The problem was raising money. We had none. I talked to a few business people about this and they pointed out that they don't always use their own money – they use other people's. We decided to borrow enough money to buy the building, and since credit unions were not ready for this type of venture, we went to the bank.

We could get a mortgage for 75 percent of the value of the property, but we needed to find the other 25 percent. To do that, board members had to sign a bank guarantee. This was a real test of commitment. Our plan was to rent parts of the building to different tenants to create income, but first we had to sign off on the down payment.

What was quite interesting was that we only began to feel like a real group when we owned assets and owed money. Eventually, we developed other projects, including a dental clinic, and formed a larger complex called New Dawn Enterprises. Our approach was problem-oriented and practical. When we identified a critical shortage of dentists in the area, we decided to acquire a building and seek a health grant from the province. We built a dental clinic and attracted a dentist from the mainland.

This taught me that a community group's chances of success are higher when its organizers put up their own money and participate in risk. Our local projects have been quite small and driven mainly by volunteers, but they have worked out quite well.

Mondragon, a flagship of the international cooperative movement, did not start as a co-op. It began with five young men who worked for a metal-fabrication company. Their local pastor had inspired them with ideas of social justice and equality, and they had also become dissatisfied with being mere employees with no control.

They met and talked about forming their own business in the early 1950s. They considered various businesses, but in Spain under Franco it was difficult to get a license to start one. Then a businessman in Vitoria, the county capital, decided to retire and sell his stove-manufacturing company. The five young men simply bought the company's shares for 400,000 *pesetas* (about US$3,500) and moved it to Mondragon to manufacture kerosene stoves. They used the money they had and borrowed the rest.

This happened in 1955, on October 20. It was a simple company and a simple business. Later, in 1959, the five friends took a letter from each of their names and formed Ulgor Cooperative.

For these five innovators the problem came first (decent jobs), then the type of business (stove manufacturing), and thirdly its structure (a co-op that suited their relationship). As they formed more businesses, Ulgor grew into the Mondragon Cooperative Corporation.

⊃ Social context

In my own situation, raising money has always been a problem. Having closely studied Mondragon, I discovered that they really began to grow when they formed a commercial credit union.

> The kind of social enterprise needed in one community may be irrelevant in another.

In the 1980s I tried to get the local credit union to finance a community-based business. It suggested that we move the New Dawn accounts to a local bank, since business was not its mandate. The credit union was dedicated to thrift and personal finance.

As an organizer, I formed a committee from New Dawn to design our own investment business. The lead person was a brilliant accountant who worked at the steel plant. I soon learned that accountants are not good at starting businesses. They like to have five years mapped out first. The committee also included teachers, social workers and a business person. Again, we talked a lot but could not come to a decision.

Finally, I recruited two business people I knew. They thought that the idea made sense. At the second meeting, we decided to lend $5,000 each to the new company. We would then ask other people we knew to put up some money as well. Eventually, we raised $500,000.

Our campaign coincided with a crisis being faced by a local group. The Reserve Mines Credit Union's building was falling down. They asked us for money, but we proposed constructing a new building in Reserve Mines town and that the credit union become a tenant. The town was quite dilapidated, so a new building would provide a shot in the arm.

The choice of business, of course, depends upon the context. Job creation is not a big necessity in a buoyant economy. In a strong economy, improving housing and working conditions and lowering the cost of living are more important. Many groups in cities across Canada have formed a variety of co-op housing projects. People could not afford housing, so groups formed, found land and built homes. In areas of high unemployment, the challenge is to create jobs, without which the community dies.

Social contexts differ greatly. The kind of social enterprise needed in one community may be irrelevant in another. The main problem in most large cities today is that many working people remain poor. Calgary is a good example. It is one of the wealthiest cities in Canada, yet those who work in some sectors, such as fast food, cannot afford the rent for accommodations. In the winter, a number of churches make their halls available during the night for the working poor. In this social context, low-cost restaurants and affordable housing are the key needs.

Affordable housing is not a problem in small communities in northern Newfoundland. Lots of people inherit the homes of their grandparents. The problem there is lack of work. In this social context, creating jobs so that people can play a constructive role in society is essential. Community activists there can identify new opportunities and then organize the commercial structures necessary to create jobs.

Businesses must be related to the local context. An analogy explains it well. Business is like a tree. If you take a royal palm tree from the tropics and plant it in Fort MacMurray, Alberta, it will die. Similarly, a business that produces energy-efficient furnaces will not succeed in Mexico but will be very useful in northern Alberta.

⮑ Brainstorming

In choosing a business, it is best to try a brainstorming session and place several potential businesses on the table. Following the place-based model, the business has to be tied to the local situation.

> As well as being rude, inquisitions are ineffective. Attitudes surface in general conversation.

When a group settles on a business that is obviously fulfilling some need, it is much easier to get support and enthusiasm. Most people like to feel that they are doing something significantly good for the local community. New Dawn started a dental business because there was a critical shortage of dentists in Cape Breton in the 1970s. By that time, we had had some experience in real estate.

The most important aspect of choosing a business is having people on the team with actual success in business. Usually social activists do not like to work with business people. I understand this. When I graduated from university, I was very uncomfortable with business people since they had money and too many people had none. However, choosing a business that has potential for success is a skill. It seems to be a kind of instinct. Consequently, it is extremely important to have some successful business people involved.

When identifying and inviting a successful business person to join the group, isms and ideologies should be cast aside. The organizers should get answers to certain questions. Is the business leader concerned about unemployment in the local area? Is he or she concerned about the lack of affordable housing? Is he or she willing to make a contribution to the community without personal financial gain?

Of course, you do not ask these questions directly. As well as being rude, inquisitions are ineffective. Attitudes surface in general conversation.

What is crucial here is that it is foolhardy for a group to attempt to start a business if its members have no experience or firsthand knowledge of business. It would be like someone trying to lead a hockey team without knowing how to skate.

Identifying Resources

Once you have identified one or two business opportunities, the next step is to survey the community for available resources. What you find will surprise you. Successful businesses depend upon the discovery of available resources. Of course, the whole notion of resource has changed over the years. This century is much more complex, especially in terms of technology and services, and the notion of a resource bears further discussion.

Although there are exceptions, such as lobsters off Nova Scotia and Newfoundland, physical resources are becoming far less important as we move into the 21st century. Keep in mind, too, that physical material becomes a resource only through the creativity and imagination of people.

Of more fundamental importance is the question of human and financial resources available to you as a founding group. Resources are always relative to a context. What is a resource in one context is not a resource in another. We can speak of material resources, but also human, cultural and financial resources.

It is quite clear that today we create many more jobs in selling services than in selling goods. The relative importance of each depends upon where we are. We must distinguish between the large metropolitan areas such as New York, Montreal and Vancouver, and the non-metropolitan areas such as Maine, Cape Breton and northern Manitoba. A small community in Maine would find a model closer to itself in northern Newfoundland than in Boston. Each group must look at its own community first and then try to find some models from similar contexts.

> Keep in mind, too, that physical material becomes a resource only through the creativity and imagination of people.

33

➲ Shifting tastes

What is important is that in our developed systems we can choose what most of our resources will be. Wealth will depend to a large

> Success will depend upon how well we are able to access general human, financial and governmental resources.

degree upon attitudes. Two generations ago, lobsters were considered to be inedible scavengers. Haddock was much more valuable. Today tastes are reversed. Lobster is much more valuable than haddock. The government of Nova Scotia recently changed the name of what we call dogfish to Northern Shark. Now, with its new official name, dogfish is destined to become a gourmet dish.

During the last 10 years the demand for fish has increased tremendously. Some authorities attribute the great surge in market demand to the health-food movement in the United States. Fish is widely believed to be healthier than red meat. Such a revolution in taste, of course, would not apply in a country where food is scarce, so we must never forget context.

In our traditional economy the obvious resources were substances such as oil, coal and minerals. Today it is more complex. For one company in the US the billions of stars that light up the heavens have become a valuable resource. An international registry of stars has been established and, for a fee, this company will let you name a star that has yet to acquire one. They provide a certificate with the astronomical location of the newly named star and enter the name in the international registry. Now, instead of giving a girlfriend a diamond, young American men are being encouraged to name stars after them. What better gift on Valentine's Day than to be given your own star?

The promoter even adds a religious value to this resource, suggesting that a star makes an excellent baptismal gift. Because of the popularity of baptismal gifts in some European countries, this company is considering opening a branch in the European Union. It sounds far-fetched but it works: customers are snapping up stars.

In post-industrial countries, especially in the many pockets of high unemployment in non-metropolitan areas and in urban areas of high-cost housing, community-business groups must go beyond physical resources. Success will depend upon how well we are able to access general human, financial and governmental resources.

What is sometimes viewed as a problem can also be a business opportunity. Distressed communities often have an unusually high percentage of older people. The young have joined the brain drain toward growing economies. However, the senior-citizen sector of a society can be a market for services.

Complexes and services for seniors can provide jobs for young people. Since their children have gone, seniors often have more disposable income. Also, retired people can be a great source of board members. Rather than wait for an international chain to provide services for seniors, it is healthier for local community businesses to control these enterprises.

○ Talent hunt

All the cases we have looked at have had a high degree of local, volunteer leadership. The success of these community-business ventures depended to a large degree upon the recruitment of quality people to serve on boards and committees. We also saw that employees were not simply employees. Even when the legal structure was quite traditional, they felt ownership and a sense of commitment to a community mission.

> When there is no highly organized system to react to problems, individual and personal participation becomes the key.

One important point to be made here concerns how things get done at the community level, especially in the face of economic decline. When there is no highly organized system to react to problems, individual and personal participation becomes the key.

It is often the case that if volunteers do not take the initiative their goal will not be reached because the technocratic systems are not in place to make it happen. In recent years, governments have simply withdrawn from some areas, such as social housing. The personal volunteer has become more essential than ever.

The human contribution, which is manifest in so many boards and committees at the local level, is also a key economic resource. In some community-based projects, local professional volunteers have been able to generate income for the group through their contributed services. This is not to be confused with selling tickets and bake sales. It means that the board members did actual work for the project, such as the drawing up of legal documents or engineering plans. The group then charged the outside customer for these services and thus added to revenue. This kind of contribution is sometimes called "sweat equity."

Universities, community colleges and high schools are a wonderful source of sweat equity. They are publicly funded and contain a vast array of technical talent in many fields. Although it is difficult for teachers to participate in and use their facilities to assist private, profit-motivated business, they can be easily involved in community-oriented business activities. Because of their training, such people are well suited to serving on boards and committees.

In many of the examples we have seen, the educational institution provided free services that were of great value in starting new enterprises. Some even used their students to assist through class projects. Such activities are great opportunities for teachers and students to become involved in the real world.

People are the greatest economic resource. There are plenty of examples of people from remote areas who developed high technical skills in a city and then returned home to start a high-tech business. One such case, for example, can be found in the Pyrenees region of Spain, where an electronic enterprise is built around one highly qualified person who prefers to live in his traditional village.

Especially in the case of high-tech industries, it appears that location is irrelevant. What is essential is highly qualified technicians. There are cases where the enterprise exists in a particular location not because of any local physical resources, nor because of any physical infrastructure, but mainly because the technical entrepreneur wishes to live there.

It is also striking how prominent the role of women has become in many of the new and emerging corporate forms. In older communities the role of women was often restricted to domestic duties, and social and church-related activities. However, in the community-business movement, there is a distinctly higher level of female participation in boards and management.

Through numerous informal activities, women often develop high levels of organizational and leadership skills. These skills then become a valuable resource when oriented towards business problems. Thus, it is important for your group to realize that many women in your area have the potential to become very effective business leaders, although they may not think of themselves that way yet.

⊃ Cultural vitality

Mondragon is a good example of dependence on human resources rather than physical ones. It is located in a remote mountainous area. There is no railway, no airport and no harbour close by, yet people there are the main manufacturers of fridges and stoves in Spain. Mondragon is obviously not built on physical resources or infrastructure.

> A region's particular culture and its history are among its key resources.

The key is found in a high level of leadership and dedication, which is rooted in local history and culture. The skill of the local people is the key resource, rather than the minerals that used to be mined in the region.

Some commentators miss the point when they dismiss the case because it is based on local loyalty rather than techniques that can be applied universally. It is true that the economic activities of large metropolitan areas are based on such techniques. However, place-based development functions differently: it is possible only if it is built on what is particular to the local area.

A region's particular culture and its history are among its key resources. If the economic rules of play prevent the local community from building on what is particular to it, then the local community is doomed to be an outpost for global economic actors.

37

In Cheticamp, a French village in an Anglophone province, a renewal of strength in traditional culture has brought about a very dynamic economic revival. The strength comes not from being the same as everyone else, but by differing from others. Their best brains and most aggressive leaders want to stay because they are part of the culture and prefer it to the dominant English culture of the metropolis. In a similar way, cultural difference could become a positive advantage for native communities.

As I have argued, economic resources are relative to a context. We make a mistake when we transfer the strategies used in large global corporations to community-business endeavours. It is a huge challenge for a developed country, organized mainly on the basis of large technocratic systems, to allow and foster local initiatives based on resources that are personalized, communal, unique and impossible to systematize.

The survival of communities, as social entities, depends upon their ability to take advantage of their own resources, mainly human and cultural ones. Their survival depends upon being able to be themselves.

This has not been the dominant policy in North America. Rather, the American approach has tended to create a homogeneous melting pot where everyone shares one language and one culture. Canada has resisted this trend to some degree.

Especially in the case of aboriginal peoples, the tendency to discourage native cultures may have contributed to the economic decline of so many native communities. In discouraging pride of culture and self-identity, government authorities may have unwittingly suppressed the kind of psychological energy that makes economic development possible.

⮑ Capital entrapment

When we examine financial resources we see that very often communities with high unemployment have a high level of capital available, but it has been channeled to outside uses.

> The problem is not a lack of capital; it is the way the capital is controlled and directed.

In many communities labour unions have hundreds of millions of dollars in their pension plans, while local people have hundreds of millions of dollars in retirement savings that take the form of bonds, investment certificates, and stocks of various kinds. The vast majority of the capital is used to fuel business development in other places.

So the problem is not a lack of capital; it is the way the capital is controlled and directed. The best example of capital entrapment for local job creation is Mondragon. Their chain of over 100 co-op banks provides the capital source for their industrial development. In Quebec, the organized labour movement has created a solidarity fund that allows workers to save, receive tax benefits and have their money used for business development in the province.

In the United States, the South Shore Bank of Chicago is an excellent example of a local bank intentionally gathering local money to be used in local development. The Cape Breton Labourers' Union fund is another example; individual workers lending 25 cents per hour created a pool of capital totaling more than $1 million. In Sydney, BCA Holdings simply asked local residents to make investor loans so that it could invest in local business. It was simple. In New Brunswick, SIMA accumulated several million dollars for local development.

It is possible to access capital in almost any community. A community business cannot succeed unless there is some friendly financial institution to provide support.

⮑ Working with governments

Normally, a corporation receives investment money from share-holders for the start-up and the operating costs of the first few

> Community-business groups should have no permanent friends and no permanent enemies in government.

years. Profits are not expected before the third or even fifth year. By their nature, community-based businesses do not have access to the same kind of capital.

However, since the community-business corporation serves the public interest, it is most appropriate that governments become involved. The money received from government is an investment rather than a grant. There is a healthy sense in which the government invests in a community business on behalf of the shareholders, who are the public. This, however, does not make the community group an agency of government. It maintains a commitment to become wealth-producing and self-sustaining in the long term.

Funding is always a contentious issue. If government provides funds in the wrong way, the whole objective of development can be defeated. Block funding is best. The group is given an amount of money and told to invest it in the best possible manner for local development. The local board decides where to invest, not government officials.

Government decisions about further funding should be based on the results of previous funding, as is usually done in conventional bank financing. This should not be construed to imply that banks can do the job and government financing is not necessary. Banks simply will not provide the initial required investment because of the risk factor normally present in the depleted communities we are considering.

Governments in most industrialized countries provide a wide variety of programs designed to promote initiatives for local employment. The variation among countries and between provinces is so wide that it is impractical to provide a guidebook.

Usually there is a distinction between assistance given to the corporation as a business and assistance given to help employees. Business assistance is usually categorized as capital grants or operating grants. Some of the government programs geared to help employees are quite creative and useful.

There are many government agencies in each area. Different agencies have different programs that can help. It is up to the board of a community business to analyze carefully the wide array of programs that can be adapted and used for their purposes. The worst programs are those that last for one year and require re-application annually. They are usually a waste of time.

When we think of government, we must clearly distinguish government officials from politicians. Some community leaders spend energy winning the favour of a politician and assume that grants will follow. This is extremely dangerous because when one politician is defeated, the victorious rival will view the community group as an opponent. Community-business groups should have no permanent friends and no permanent enemies in government. It is best to deal with government officials first and then give credit to the government, regardless of its political stripe.

Most important of all, the group must not become completely dependent on government. Success is unlikely if it cannot raise private money in the local community.

41

Legal Structure

After looking at a wide variety of community business, there appears to be a general agreement on a set of basic values, even though these values usually remain implicit. However, there is no clear agreement on what the best structure is.

Once the group has decided that it wishes to launch a business, a legal structure has to be chosen. Those who come from a conventional business background will automatically choose the structure of a joint stock company where the enterprise is controlled by whoever holds the majority of its shares. Those who come from a social background will automatically choose a cooperative structure in which each person has one vote regardless of the number of shares owned.

For many, the structure is symbolic. It is a kind of flag representing a tradition. The danger here is that people become dedicated and loyal to a particular structure rather than a particular purpose. The healthiest attitude is to regard the legal structure as a tool, rather than an end in itself.

Joint stock companies and cooperatives are organizational tools. Tools are meant to be used to get something done. It seems logical to me that I start not with the tool, but with the purpose and the practical problem I want to solve.

Credit union co-ops have been very successful in Canada. Social activists have been enthusiastic about expanding credit unions. However, it is unclear what problem credit unions are supposed to solve. I would certainly prefer to see more credit unions than more global banks. However, I am disappointed when I see TV ads urging me to use a credit union because its staff is friendlier. Every corporation in the world claims that it is friendly!

> The danger here is that people become dedicated and loyal to a particular structure rather than a particular purpose.

⊃ Goals

There have been many movements to improve society. The cooperative movement is one that comes to mind immediately. It has improved the lives

> If business development is the goal, a large number of people can be a hindrance and a nuisance.

of many people over the years. Impressed by past achievements, enthusiasts today often begin organizing to form co-ops.

However, they are often unclear about what the co-op should do. This is like forming a club in order to have a club, without being clear about its purpose or day-to-day activity. As mentioned earlier, organizations of any kind are tools for getting something done.

It is fairly easy to attract generous people to a meeting if the objective is simply getting some houses built when there is an apparent need for houses. It is harder to get them to come if the objective is to form do-gooder organizations or to improve society in general.

Some organizations may be for simple entertainment and personal development. Some may be for advocacy, while others may be for business development. The advocacy organization will be very different from one set up to develop a job-creating business for the unemployed. In advocacy, a high percentage of the local population must be involved. Mass participation is the only way to achieve a political impact. However, if business development is the goal, a large number of people can be a hindrance and a nuisance.

In house-building, for example, the involvement of too many people can cause inefficiency and the loss of money. Is the group mainly concerned about getting houses built, or teaching people about the housing industry? Teaching about housing and actually building houses are very different activities requiring different tools.

Instead of deciding to form a cooperative or a joint stock company, I find that it is better to begin by deciding to form a business to respond to local needs. This is a very different psychological attitude. The particular structure of any organization is a means to an end. In a healthy lifestyle, money is a means to obtain goods and services. In a disordered life, money becomes an end in itself. Some people accumulate money, valuing it in itself and forgetting that it is a tool to be used for something. The tool must fit the problem, and this brings us into the forms of organization that can be useful.

In the case of community enterprise, there are three kinds of business incorporation. Some groups start out as an association under the Society's Act of their area, but when a group begins to do business it is extremely important to become incorporated under more appropriate legislation. The reason for this is that a society does not enjoy "limited liability."

When a group has limited liability the assets of the private citizen are not at risk in the case of a lawsuit. If a society or association carries on a business and is sued, then individual members can be charged and their assets seized. Under most legal systems, associations and societies are not designed for operating businesses. The legislation of most jurisdictions grants limited liability only to businesses incorporated under a Company's Act or a Cooperative's Act. The three typical forms of incorporation are: a joint stock company, a cooperative company and a not-for-profit company (sometimes called a company limited by guarantee).

➲ Joint stock companies

The vast majority of businesses in the Western world are organized as joint stock companies under a Company's Act. This means that the shares of the company are owned by individuals.

> In effect, a joint stock company can operate as a cooperative.

Each share has a vote, so that an individual with 100 shares would have 100 votes, while the one with 50 shares would have 50 votes. Individuals normally have the right to sell their shares on the open market.

Community-business corporations organized as joint stock companies, such as GNP in Newfoundland, normally try to prevent outside buy-outs by passing a shareholders' resolution that bars shareholders from selling to outside interests. In some cases where the objective is communitarian, shareholders enter into legal agreements that limit each person to one vote regardless of the number of shares owned. In effect, a joint stock company can operate as a cooperative.

⊃ Cooperatives

The more traditional form of community enterprise is through the cooperative legal structure. The two traditional forms are consumer and producer co-ops. The famous Rochdale co-op, and most co-ops in the Western world, are consumer co-ops engaged in retail, marketing and financial businesses.

> The new and emerging kind of development co-op is multi-functional and integrated.

Mondragon is an exception. It is mainly a system of producer or worker co-ops. The consumer co-op is controlled by the customer and the producer co-op by its worker-members. Co-ops normally distribute surplus revenue to their members at the end of each year. At Mondragon, for example, they do not speak of wages, but prefer terms such as "anticipated revenues."

Most legal jurisdictions have a Cooperative's Act, but the technical conditions vary. Normally, co-ops enjoy limited liability and members can sell their shares. However, there is only one vote per person. As in any organization, the members elect a board and the board chooses the manager, who will act as chief executive officer.

In recent years there have been new co-op forms dedicated to general community economic development rather than to one specific service. The best example is the Regional Development Cooperative in Quebec. It groups a variety of co-ops in order to pool resources for local development.

Traditionally, most co-ops were uni-functional: they carried out finance as a credit union; sold consumer goods, such as Atlantic Co-op; or caught and sold fish, such as a fishery co-op. The new and emerging kind of development co-op is multifunctional and integrated. It seeks to take on whatever kind of economic tasks a community requires.

According to cooperative legislation, each member owns a share and therefore a percentage of the company's assets. Normally, the members have the right to sell the assets and divide the revenue among the members. For this reason, a co-op is usually subject to income tax. But this tax liability is often contested by co-ops by virtue of the community service they perform.

⊃ Not-for-profit companies

Most Western countries have a not-for-profit form of incorporation. In some jurisdictions, it is called a company limited by guarantee and in others it is called a Part Two company. In this structure, there are members rather than shareholders. It is normally covered in a subsection of the Company's Act.

> I consider the not-for-profit community-business corporation to be an evolved cooperative.

In Canada, New Dawn is a good example of a not-for-profit company. The form is much more common in Great Britain. Most of the community enterprises in Scotland are organized this way. Through this form of business incorporation there are no public shares to be bought and sold, and the rule is one vote per person. Such a corporation can make profits, but all profits must be reinvested in similar local ventures.

Normally, the memorandum of association states that the purpose of the company is community betterment and that members do not receive unearned benefits. The members serve *"pro bono publico"* – for the common good. In effect, I consider the not-for-profit community-business corporation to be an evolved cooperative. In its best sense, the word "cooperative" implies solidarity with the community and commitment to community improvement.

A person becomes a member of such a corporation upon signing the memorandum of association after fulfilling the membership requirements stipulated in the by-laws. The company enjoys limited liability, with each member promising to provide an amount of money, say $10, to it. If a corporation is designed in this manner it normally is not required to pay income tax, although an income tax form must be filed.

Typically, company taxes are related to payment of dividends by companies. The lack of dividends in a not-for-profit means that taxes are not paid. In some jurisdictions, cooperatives can be organized on a profit-making or non-profit basis.

A company limited by guarantee, like a cooperative or joint stock company, can operate as any other commercial company. It can also own profit-oriented subsidiaries, as New Dawn owns New Dawn Holdings Ltd. Many organizers prefer this kind of incorporation because it offers a great deal of business flexibility as well as the greatest legal safeguard against takeover by an outside company.

This is an important consideration because there have been cases where community-minded individuals formed a co-op, but after they died their successors sold off the business to outsiders for the sake of profit. Normally, a co-op can be bought out by another one unless there is a special article in its by-laws. A not-for-profit cannot be bought out, so it is really anchored in the local area.

Any of the above corporate forms can be adapted and used to carry on business dedicated to community improvement. When the founders of Mondragon started, their aim was to initiate a democratic, community-based business. After proceeding, they found that the cooperative structure was the most suitable, although it did not completely fulfill their needs. In normal cooperative structures, the surplus revenue belongs to shareholders who have the right to withdraw this money as dividends. Mondragon departed from this tradition by ruling that 20 percent of the surplus belongs to the business itself. This became a very effective means of self-capitalization.

➲ Opt for flexibility

What is important is that the group chooses a legal structure that allows the most flexibility in achieving its purposes. It is very important that the group conceive of itself as multifunctional. It is a mistake to make a rigid structure suitable for only one kind of business, such as selling

> It is important to reformulate principles for economic action because the context is constantly changing.

groceries or building houses. It can happen that the group may begin with something very specific, such as a housing project, but find later that it wishes to pursue a new opportunity and that its legal structure does not allow for this.

It is quite clear that the notion of a community-business corporation includes the capacity to evolve and adapt to any economic need or opportunity that may arise. By its nature it must be a multifunctional business if it is to be an enabling structure giving the community more capacity to control its economic destiny.

An attractive definition, incorporating many of the ideas discussed above, was drafted by an organization called Community Business Scotland in 1982:

"A community business is a trading organization which is owned and controlled by the local community and which aims to create ultimately self-supporting and viable jobs for local people in its area of benefit, and to use profits made from its business activities either to create more employment or to provide local services, or to support local charitable works. A community business is likely to have a multi-purpose enterprise and it may be based on a geographical community or on a community of interest." [*]

Taking a cue from this, I suggest that the corporate community business model be based on a number of principles. Let us remember that it is important to reformulate principles for economic action because the context is constantly changing.

In the 19th century, calls for a democratic process were revolutionary because the wider society accepted an aristocratic model of control. Calls for democratic action were part of the language for change.

Today, however, almost every institution claims to be in favour of democracy. (The United States invaded Iraq in the name of democracy.) It would be most unusual to hear any contemporary organization claim that they did not favour democracy. The word has become almost as meaningless as George Orwell forewarned in his novel *1984*.

---

[*] Calouste Gulbenkian Foundation, UK Branch, *Community Business Works: A Report by the Calouste Gulbenkian Foundation*, page 4.

The following are some guiding principles that help characterize the community corporation:

> **Trustee of the Community**: It should conceive of itself as a trustee of community interest rather than the interest of any one specific group. In the sense of accountability it should be similar to universities or hospitals, which are normally governed by trustee boards. There should be members but no shareholders. It should clearly have the mission of serving and developing the geographic community it is located in.

> **Priority of the Local**: Rather than have workers relocate to where a business is, it would move the business to their community.

> **Participation**: Members are those who are actively carrying out its purposes. They are employees as well as volunteers from the community who serve on boards and committees. Participation is the criterion for membership. The organization is controlled democratically by the associated members and representatives of the local community. Ownership of a paper share hardly implies participation.

> **Universalism**: It will cooperate with and form consortia with other like-minded co-op corporations to form first a locally integrated system, then a regional one, and finally a world system. The principle of subsidiary would be adopted so that the maximum authority and function is devolved to lower levels with power moving up the hierarchy only when it is beyond the capacity of lower levels.

> **Growth Oriented**: It will be growth oriented as long as unemployment exists in its region.

> **Wage Solidarity**: It adopts a policy of wage solidarity, such that a percentage of net earnings is distributed to employee-members in a proportionate manner, and percentages retained as non-divisible public equity for local development.

> **Not-For-Profit**: It would be not-for-profit in the sense that profit is the means to achieve its long-term purposes.

> **Multifunctional**: It would be multifunctional, innovative and flexible since local needs are diverse and change over time.

In some ways the first two principles above could describe the manner in which universities were once organized. In most countries, universities were corporations controlled by the people who worked in them. Although we never spoke of the professors as owning the university, the concept of a group of people controlling the university as a public trust was commonly accepted. Hospitals are usually considered to be a similar kind of trust.

Of course, such service corporations are radically different from business corporations where operational systems are based on market forces. Education based on market forces would be disastrous for those of us who believe in universal human rights. However, the adaptation of a retail co-op to market forces makes sense.

According to the prestigious British legal expert L.C.B. Gower, "A company is a group of individuals joined in pursuit of a common activity... usually economic gain." He points out that ownership of large corporations by shareholders is a legal fiction:

"A holder of 100 shares in, say, Imperial Chemical Industries is a member of the company but it is a fantasy to describe him as associating with the other members in running it. The running of the business is left to the directors, or probably to the managing directors, and the shareholder, although a member, is in economic reality, but not in the eyes of the law, a mere lender of capital, on which he hopes for a return but without any effective control over the borrower." *

Traditional cooperatives appear to have come closest to the original sense of "corporation" as a public trust rather than simply shareholder ownership. We use the term "trustee" to suggest stewardship rather than ownership.

As pointed out by Berle and Means: "Few American enterprises, and no large corporations, can take the view that their plants, tools and organizations are their own, and that they can do what they please with them as their own. There is increasing recognition of the fact that collective operations, and those

---

* L.C.B. Gower, *The Principles of Modern Company Law*, page 9.

predominantly conducted by large corporations, are like operations carried on by the state itself. Corporations are essentially political constructs." *

Hence, the common good – society at large – has a stake in, and must have a say in, the manner in which community businesses are structured. In a very real way, the business corporation is a trust representing a variety of interests or stakeholders: the managers, the lenders, the workers, the community and the government, as well as the suppliers of capital. All must be represented in the governance of a business corporation. This approach is sometimes called "stakeholder theory."

This priority of the local is obviously in contrast to our understanding of capitalistic mobility, carried over from the industrial revolution, when workers were expected to leave their communities and move to where the factories were. Yet, in the Western world, where 80 percent of jobs are in the service sector, there should be much more choice in location. **

Many communities in the West are veritable ghost towns because of forced migration: people have to leave to find jobs. We ought to follow the principle that the economy must adapt to people and not force people to adapt to it.

⊃ Ethical growth

Our fourth principle, universalism, is based on a more optimistic notion of the global market system. Despite the known problems of

> Instead of strong nations exploiting weak ones, we aim for an economic system of mutual collaboration.

global exploitation, we must assume that world trade is here to stay and that it can be a positive force for human improvement.

But instead of strong nations exploiting weak ones, we aim for an economic system of mutual collaboration, with the present cooperative business sector leading the way towards a new kind of internationalism in business.

---

* Adolph Berle and Gardiner Means, *The Modern Corporation and Private Property*, page xxvi.

** Thad Williamson, David Imbrosscio and Gar Alperovitz, *Making a Place for Community: Local Democracy in a Global Era.*

This characterization was emphasized at the International Cooperative Alliance meeting in Manchester (1988). Cooperatives were encouraged to collaborate with other cooperatives. Alone, a business may be weak, but united all become stronger.

Capitalist companies long ago learned the commercial benefits of merging. The Emilia Romagna complex in Italy has developed very effective structures to attain commercial advantage by forming a variety of consortia among local co-ops. The unemployment rate in their region is 4 percent, the lowest in Italy. In my view, cooperative corporations should begin by collaborating in their local community and then continue collaborating at the national and international levels.

According to the fifth principle, growth can be regarded as an ethical obligation. In view of the enormous problems of unemployment, poverty and general inequality in the world, the power of the agent of change would have to be commensurate with the size of the problem. Because we operate in a market economy, an ability to influence the operations of the market will depend upon the size of the corporation.

For example, many early retail cooperatives were able to reduce the general cost of groceries in a local market simply by entering the market system. The local retail cooperative prevented exploitation by the local grocery barons because they were big enough to compete.

Because of its size, the Mondragon complex is able to set job-creation targets of 3,000-4,000 new workers each year. Small-scale businesses can be wonderful for personal growth and human relationships, but any business system that wishes to influence world markets must become big.

⊃ Profits and innovation

The wage principle relates to retained earnings or profits, which has always been a subject for debate in socially oriented businesses. The old argument as to whether workers or capitalists deserve the

> Diversity in a business helps assure survival and sustainability.

surplus value does not make much sense today. Retained earnings, added value or profit are not simply attributed to workers, management or owners of capital; productivity is the result of complex relationships between many elements in society.

Thus, we suggest that earnings be divided – the proportions will depend upon local circumstances and culture. Obviously some retained earnings should be used as incentives for good work, but the main objective for retained earnings should be for reinvestment and growth for the business as such. These retained, indivisible earnings could well be called public or community equity.

While profit has become a pejorative word because of a long history of corporate exploitation, the notion of profit as a measure of efficiency has been very useful in the world of business. When community groups attempt to carry on business without making a profit and without suffering a loss, they usually go bankrupt, thus the term not-for-profit. According to this concept, profit is a means of success, a way to further develop the business. In a for-profit business, profit itself is the purpose.

The last principle is related to the Knowledge Economy, where innovation is a key factor for business success.* Innovation implies flexibility in structure and product. We sometimes use the term "multifunctional" in that sense. Most community groups that start businesses for social purposes tend to choose just one function (e.g. a housing business or a grocery business), whereas a multifunctional business can adapt to changing contexts.

Over time, some functions will no longer be needed and new ones can be added, allowing long-term continuity of the business. For this reason, a tobacco company might attempt to diversify by buying a toothpaste company. Diversity in a business helps assure survival and sustainability. From a social point of view, it allows the business to better serve society.

These reflections on community-based businesses are meant to stimulate debate in a process of rethinking what they do. They are ideas based on

---

* Jane Marceau, "Clusters, Chains, and Complexes: Three Approaches to Innovation with a Public Policy Perspective," in *Handbook of Industrial Innovation*, pages 3-12.

observation of practice. There is no one example in the world that fulfills our ideal perfectly; however, some come more or less closer to it. Where Mondragon epitomizes the notion of members associating in a common task, Emilia Romagna is a fine example of cooperation among co-ops. New Dawn and BCA Holdings in Cape Breton are cooperatives without shares. Quebec has a whole variety of innovative experiments such as their worker-shareholder co-ops, as distinct from worker co-ops, and their regional development co-ops.*

Many more experiments are needed to find forms and structures that will allow the development of a strong community-based business sector able to act as a major force for economic justice in the world.

What is key here is the notion that all structures are relative. What is constant is the community purpose. The group must seek a legal structure that protects and ensures that the long-term purpose will be carried out even after the founders have passed on.

---

* Daniel Côté et Andrée-Anne Gratton. *La Coopérative de Développement Régional de la Région de Québec.*

Launching the Business

Now it is time for a detailed analysis of the one or two business opportunities your group has settled on. After reaching consensus on the question of a legal structure, there are now some very practical problems that must be faced.

How do you actually launch a business? The first temptation is to hire a large consulting firm to do a business feasibility study. However, in most of the successful cases I have seen that wasn't done. Also, it appears that most conventional businesses didn't start that way. In the more successful cases, the founding board does some of the feasibility study itself, sometimes using sub-committees. Often a small amount of money is spent on a consultant.

The model wherein a group awards a major contract to outside consultants who return with a blueprint for action is rare. I think that the value of feasibility studies has been greatly overrated by community-business groups. A dedicated board member who has been successful and understands the ups and downs of real-life business is more valuable than a consulting firm.

The complexity of beginning the project can vary widely. At New Dawn we purchased and renovated a building. The Great Northern Peninsula Development Corporation took over a fish-processing plant.

> I think that the value of feasibility studies has been greatly overrated by community-business groups.

⊃ Move quickly

Most people become discouraged if a great deal of time is spent talking without results. They simply will not stay with the community-business group. It seems quite obvious that it is easier when the beginning is small and modest. Of course, the simplest approach is to take over an existing business that is already operational.

> There is nothing like a track record to establish credibility.

In order to make a start, the initial board and/or the initial organization may have to provide seed capital in the form of a loan or bank guarantee. Once a start has been made and cashflow established, then it is much easier to plan larger and more ambitious enterprises. There is nothing like a track record to establish credibility.

Some groups plan huge projects that take years to develop. Most often, such groups fade away because there are no short-term results to encourage their efforts. Moreover, large projects require expensive and complicated feasibility studies, something inexperienced groups should avoid. However, this does not mean we should confine ourselves to small projects. Rather, the lesson is that a modest beginning is best as a learning experience.

Once established, the group should move on to larger enterprises. In a region marred by economic decline and high unemployment, expansion and growth are moral obligations.

⊃ Managing growth

As the small business project develops and the group has proven its commitment, extensive efforts should be made to recruit the best business and technical resources in the area.

> Collaboration with existing and like-minded businesses is vital.

As noted earlier, a university or community college is an excellent source of talent and skill. My experience shows that competent business people are often well disposed to volunteer their services if the organizing group is serious about initiating real business with all the usual control systems.

At this point, it is worth repeating that the role of the board is fundamentally one of monitoring and giving direction. It is not the job of the board to make day-to-day decisions. That is the role of management. A danger in many community-based businesses is that board members try to obtain jobs for their friends and relatives. Picking staff is the role of management. Furthermore, a board should not be concerned about learning to draft a business plan or a balance sheet. These are staff functions.

If the new staff is small and lacks these skills, then they should contract them out. If the group has a relationship with a college or a university, then these functions can be carried out by one of the professors on a volunteer basis.

In launching a community business, the same rules apply that guide any individuals starting a business. It is essential that the structure be open and flexible to allow for a variety of subsidiaries and departments so that the business can become multifunctional.

In the case of a community business, collaboration with existing and like-minded businesses is vital. Many community businesses, such as housing and retail co-ops, see themselves as restricted to a single business activity. A housing co-op builds houses and that is all. Or a grocery co-op sells groceries and that is all. However, as pointed out earlier, orphan businesses are as fragile as the label suggests.

If community-oriented businesses already exist in the area, the group should attempt to establish alliances and partnerships. There is no sense in trying to reinvent the wheel. Some credit unions offer low-interest loans to groups starting a community business. Some universities will allow community businesses to use their facilities. Moreover, some institutions have very helpful programs for the formation and updating of management and staff.

Such solidarity and collaboration is fundamental in the community-business movement and will facilitate a start-up. New Deal was launched with the assistance of New Dawn Enterprises; Old Barrel Potato Chip Co was launched with the help of the local credit union; Tompkins Development was started with the help of BCA Holdings.

⊃ M&As

Mergers and acquisitions have become ubiquitous in the conventional business world, and the practice can be used to great advantage in the community-business sector. For instance,

> It is much simpler to purchase or gain control of an existing company.

BCA Holdings saw an opportunity in its community when a rope company went bankrupt and was in danger of being purchased by an outside company. The sale to an outside firm would have meant the loss of jobs as well as local tax revenue. BCA competed and bought the company. Local investors were recruited to buy shares and the company was made operational. Workers were invited to become shareholders. They declined, preferring the conventional labour union structure.

In a sense, the Regional Development Cooperative in the Quebec City region carried out a form of acquisition. When a manufacturing company was in difficulty, it helped the workers form a co-op. The co-op then purchased a percentage of the shares to form a worker-shareholder company.

New businesses are very difficult to launch. It was much simpler back in the 1930s when small groups in small communities could get together and set up a fishery co-op. In the case of housing, miners could use their natural skills and build a dozen houses as a cooperative. Today, the challenges are much more complex due to building codes, large global companies with local branches, myriad government regulations, etc. Amateurs are often at a loss in modern systems. That is why it is much simpler to purchase or gain control of an existing company.

In this context, one of the most important elements for success will be management. Social activists usually underestimate the role of the manager. The manager of the community business must have all the skills that any modern manager has, including the people skills necessary to keep his board involved and on side.

⊃   The organic approach

A very insightful economic geographer argues that businesses are like plants. A cactus plant grows very well in a tropical climate but not in a northern climate, just as spruce trees do not thrive in Mexico.

> Any sound business has to adapt to the local culture if it wishes to succeed.

The parallel in business is that some businesses suit some areas and some do not. For instance, in an area with a long industrial tradition, such as coal mining and metal factories, the average worker will be comfortable in manual trades. In general, however, unemployed coal miners cannot easily be trained to work in software companies, and it would be hard to train unemployed civil servants in a capital city to work in a metal-fabrication plant. Any sound business has to adapt to the local culture if it wishes to succeed.

An organic approach is also useful in financial planning. A tree will die if it does not get enough water; also, it will die if it gets too much water. In business, money is like water. If a business does not get enough money it will go bankrupt; if it gets too much money it can go bankrupt. The latter seems odd, but it is true.

I know of a person who decided to start an inn with a restaurant. He had an architect design a beautiful complex. The project cost $2 million. The government provided $1 million as a non-repayable grant. The entrepreneur then took out a mortgage of $500,000, used $250,000 of his own money and borrowed the other $250,000. It looked like a great deal because he received $1 million for free.

After two years, however, he found that he was not making enough money to pay his mortgage. The mortgage company foreclosed. The mistake was that he had plenty of money, so he overbuilt. If he had received half a million dollars as a grant and had borrowed only $250,000, he would have ended up with a tourism complex worth $1 million instead of $2 million. It would have been a simpler structure, but he could have survived.

In a poor area of Mexico, I was involved with *campesino* (farmer) business development. The group had built *tortilla* (corn bread) shops using some aid money from Canada. These were quite successful, easy to manage and met a local market need. The group rightly decided to develop a tourism business. They wanted to build some simple native cabins for tourists. After seeking help from different sources, they had some amazingly good luck. An American foundation offered them over US$500,000 to build a beautiful restaurant and cabins with modern appliances.

This looked like a wonderful opportunity. In a democratic spirit of non-interference, the foundation allowed the local group to develop the project independently. Instead of hiring a conventional contractor, they made it a community project. Their intentions were great – the *campesinos* could control the construction.

However, many construction mistakes were made. They used up all the foundation's money and to complete the project had to borrow close to US$100,000. They assumed they would soon have revenue flowing in and would be able to pay off the debt.

Unfortunately, they were not very efficient in business; revenue was low and they could not pay the debt. The project almost went bankrupt and they then faced the loss of their successful *tortilla* shops. A generous amount of money with no strings attached is not always helpful in business.

Bankrupt businesses are a tragedy for the owners, but they can be a boon for community groups. In the case of the bankrupt tourist complex, a community group bought it for $300,000. Today, it is a thriving cornerstone business in a small community. Bankrupt businesses can provide a great opportunity for fledgling community groups.

It is often helpful to return to the idea of necessary but not sufficient factors. Financial capital is necessary for business development, but it is not sufficient. Competent management is a necessary factor but not sufficient.

The two most important elements required for community groups to develop a successful business are adequate capital and competent management.

⊃ Pitfalls

Some dangers I have already pointed out. Another is the failure to distinguish between capital and operating budgets. A capital

> Without assets, a community-business group will always be weak, chasing after governments every year for a grant.

budget pays for buildings and machinery. An operating budget pays the staff and current expenses: it keeps the business going from day to day.

Especially in the field of tourism, community businesses make big mistakes. I have seen groups seek large grants from government to construct beautiful buildings. That meets their capital budget, but not their operating budget. A community group can, for example, receive $2 million from the government to build a cultural centre as part of a tourism business. It seems wonderful, but after two years the group may discover that it lacks the money to pay staff, taxes and insurance.

Rather than receive $2 million in free cash, the community would have been better served with an endowment of $500,000. It seems odd to prefer to receive $500,000 rather than $2 million. However, the half million invested can provide an income of $30,000 per year indefinitely. The group may have to use an abandoned school building or a church hall, but it will have stability.

Community groups can often appeal to local volunteers who can help renovate an old building. The new $2 million building looks very tempting, but it does not provide long-term sustainability unless there is another source of income. Moreover, tourists from New York, London and Paris do not visit local communities to look at fancy buildings – they come to sample local culture. Sometimes, an old building fixed up with taste and imagination can be much more valuable than a generic brick and glass structure.

Another temptation is to take a short-term rather than long-term view. Imagine a local development group that finds that it has accumulated $50,000 in its account as a result of some successful projects. In such a case, many groups might spend this to hire staff and provide jobs. A long-term approach is to build up assets.

This would mean that the group would use $25,000 to increase staff, perhaps on a part-time basis, and then use the remaining $25,000 to buy a building worth $100,000. The $25,000 can serve as a down payment and a local credit union could provide a $75,000 mortgage. The building could be rented and gradually the mortgage would be paid off. Eventually, the group will own the asset outright. Without assets, a community-business group will always be weak, chasing after governments every year for a grant.

Assets allow the community-business group to generate its own income. From the beginning, every community-business group should think about how it can survive for five or 10 years.

⮑ Board and manager

There is one danger that seems to be inherent in community business: the relationship between the board and the manager. When the business has

> It is very important that the board of directors have periodic meetings at which the manager is not present.

grown and the manager has been in place for a number of years, the volunteer board will assume that the manager knows best. Especially if there has been some success, the manager can become overconfident and too adventurous. Experienced board members may see the danger, but they may not want to oppose the manager.

For instance, I know of a community business that was successful in services such as landscaping and gardening supplies. The margins in their business were modest, but adequate for sustainability. However, someone came up with the idea of a purchasing a factory. The product does not matter, but in that kind of business the margins are very good and high returns can be generated. The business, however, never got off the ground, though it cost the group a lot of money. The venture was simply not suitable. Manufacturing is a capital-intensive business that requires a special kind of management.

Some board members did not want to engage in manufacturing, but they did not want to oppose the manager. Managers can excel in one kind of business but falter in another. Moreover, a certain type of manager may be necessary during the first five years of a business, but when the business gets established another type may be required. A manager whose entrepreneurial spirit has been a driving force behind a community start-up can be especially difficult for a board to oppose.

Balance between board and management is also a problem in large business corporations. Often the managers run them and the board is merely a rubber-stamp. Whatever the type of business, it is very important that the board of directors have periodic meetings at which the manager is not present. These should be scheduled, so that it is not seen as a witch hunt to get rid of the manager.

A rule can be established that the first or the final board meeting of the year is held without the manager's presence. Also, it is very useful for a board to have periodic external evaluations. Objective assessment is very useful for any board and should not be seen as a lack of confidence in the manager. It is normal business practice.

⊃ Maintaining balance

After the business has operated for a few years, the board should keep asking this question: "If we closed down our business, sold all our assets this year and paid off all of our debts, how much money would be left on the table?" If money remains, business success has been achieved. If no money remains, business success has not been achieved.

> There is no perfect person, there is no perfect organization and there is no perfect business.

It may seem terribly capitalistic to some that I insist upon the build-up of assets that are worth money. My answer is that we need tools if we wish to respond realistically to community needs. Money is simply a tool. It can be used to do good or bad. In the domain of community business it is clearly a basic necessity.

When I put on my social activist cap, I see many things that need to be done – the poor people on this street really need help. Then, when I put on my business cap, I see a different set of things that need to be done – without new sources of income we will not have enough money to pay our staff.

This friction is typical in community-business groups. It is normal. I call the one a social imperative and the other a business imperative. In the world of action, the social imperative and the business imperative are always in tension, if not conflict.

There is no perfect person, there is no perfect organization and there is no perfect business. That is what it means to be human. The everlasting challenge for community business is to find a balance between the social imperative and the business imperative.

Five Pillars

Because many communities lack infrastructure for business development, we have to establish it ourselves. This observation is based on decades of analysis of successful community-based enterprises discussed in the previous chapters: New Dawn and BCA in Atlantic Canada, and Mondragon in the Basque region of Spain. The focus in these cases is "place-based development," which sees the local context as the starting point for social change rather than a nation or the global system. Many social activists believe that changes made at the local level may eventually alter the larger context. In the cases cited above successful development depended upon five pillars: formation, finance, research, technology and government.

These five pillars are inter-related and the relationship between them is dynamic. Although each is vital, no one factor is sufficient for success. It is helpful to reiterate this distinction. In business, finance is necessary but not sufficient. Having deep pockets does not guarantee success if, say, there is a failure to understand and use the latest technology.

The relationship between these five pillars is critical. It is possible to have all five in one place, but if they are not connected, nothing happens. You can have electricity and a stereo, but if you do not plug in the stereo there will be no music. Business development occurs when the relationship between these pillars reinforces each one.

➲ Formation

Fifty years ago, it was possible to organize fishermen in a small community to form a self-managed cooperative. Very few skills were needed. However,

> The development of competent managers is an enormous challenge in economically distressed communities.

in the global economy, all businesses face international competition and highly skilled managers have become a prerequisite for forming a successful business. Forming a business has become increasingly complex due to other factors as well. Nations, for example, have become increasingly regulated: they have more rules than they did 50 years ago. If a business manager lacks knowledge of government regulations and tax laws, then that business will fail. Even managers of a small business need skills and knowledge, such how to use of the Internet to find information, that were not required 20 years ago.

The phrase "information economy" reflects the new importance of information in business. Rapid changes in science and technology also affect every business. This is why large corporations invest in research and development departments. Small businesses in small communities, however, cannot afford such departments. In most cases where community enterprises succeeded, this need was fulfilled by local schools, colleges or universities.

It is not true that everybody can do everything. Unique talents, and special training and education are required for managers nowadays. The development of competent managers is an enormous challenge in economically distressed communities.

⊃ Finance

Every country has capital located in large financial institutions, but most investment companies tend to invest in companies within 200 kilometres of their headquarters. For a business that is not located in a major city it is very difficult to attract investment. This is why Mondragon developed its own investment bank located within its community. (www. mondragon.mcc.es)

> No matter how poor a community is, it always has some capital. The hurdles to mobilizing capital are a lack of motivation and organization.

On a much smaller scale, BCA Group was set up in Cape Breton to raise money in the community for local investment. No matter how poor a community is, it always has some capital. The hurdles to mobilizing capital are a lack of motivation and organization. (www.ced.ca)

Research

Wherever there are people, there are business opportunities. Goods and services need to be exchanged. The problem is pinpointing the opportunities. This is why research is critical. In most cases of

> It is pointless to develop a new product and then discover that someone on the other side of the world has developed the same product with better technology and can sell it at a cheaper price.

successful community enterprises, a research centre was established to discover and develop business. These "action research centres" are not set up to publish articles; their key output is establishing new businesses.

The research centre should be located in the local area so that it can have a deep understanding of the local context. A business research centre in New York for example, will have a difficult time gauging the local context of the Basque region of Spain or Cape Breton. While understanding the local context is vital, the global context cannot be ignored. For example, it is pointless to develop a new product and then discover that someone on the other side of the world has developed the same product with better technology and can sell it at a cheaper price. In today's economy, it is important to be connected to international networks. This does not happen automatically. Effective business managers are usually quite busy, so special institutions or centres are required for business action research.

Technology

From the outset Mondragon's founders sought the best technology in the world for their new businesses. This practice became a major source of their success. However, it is important

> How a business is organized and how it relates to other businesses and support systems can be called "organizational technology."

to keep in mind that technology extends beyond machinery to include organization. How a business is organized and how it relates to other businesses and support systems can be called "organizational technology." Mondragon includes more than 100 enterprises, but they are linked by one marketing system, one research system and one financial system. The client companies of the Mondragon bank are monitored. Every client must present a five-year budget and monthly profit and loss statements. When the central program detects problems, an inspector is authorized to suggest solutions to the client to prevent losses.

This is a kind of technology that can prevent financial problems from spiraling out of control. If the client does not agree to the system, the loan is refused. On much smaller scale in Cape Breton, we have four finance companies in the BCA Group that are linked to our business action research centre.

⊃ Government

It is a huge mistake to think that government has no role to play. It is extremely difficult to develop any kind of business if the government is hostile. Often governments have programs to assist small businesses.

> It is usually best to place a priority on establishing a good relationship with the municipal government because it is closest to the community.

It pays to establish good relationships with all levels of government.

Conversely, it is not prudent to become identified with a single political party. It is also useful for community-based business groups to make policy presentations to government. Taxation policies and other regulations can make the difference between success and failure. In general, governments are eager to see citizen volunteers taking responsibility for job creation and business development. It is usually best to place a priority on establishing a good relationship with the municipal government because it is closest to the community.

The method of building business outlined here contrasts with economic research that creates generic models that can be implemented anywhere. The results of this research can be sold to the highest bidder. The kind of organization outlined above is directed to benefit a local community. Its purpose is to harness existing resources, along with science and technology, to develop local businesses.

⊃ The human element

I have argued that the five pillars can bring about business success if they are linked dynamically. This need for a dynamic relationship brings us back to the need for an elusive human element: leadership. Leadership involves personal motivation, energy and talent. Every community includes people with energy and talent, but what motivates people to create and social enterprises?

The so-called Chicago School of Economics argues that "greed" is the most effective motivator. Whether or not this is true, it is obvious that those whose main motivation is increasing their wealth usually choose to live where they can make the most money.

The most common motivation for business is personal profit. The so-called Chicago School of Economics argues that "greed" is the most effective motivator. Whether or not this is true, it is obvious that those whose main motivation is increasing their wealth usually choose to live where they can make the most money.

In economically distressed economies, the most successful motivation for the creation of community businesses is a moral commitment to the community. This kind of personal commitment to fellow human beings energized leaders such as Mohammad Yunus in Bangladesh and Don Jose Maria in Spain. Few can attain their level of leadership, but I have observed that every economically distressed community I have spent time in has potential leaders. All that is required is to find and encourage them. Morally committed leadership, along with the five pillars, may be the sufficient cause for a thriving community-enterprise economy.

Developing Context

Although this guide has stressed the local community as the starting point for social change, we cannot ignore the radical global shift that is contributing to the marginalization of local

> Governments continue to bend over backwards to provide incentives for metropolitan growth and centralization, arguing that this sparks economic expansion and higher national incomes.

communities: the increasing proliferation of mega-cities. Behind this trend lies a technocratic mindset that is, for the most part, taken for granted even though its consequences and the mega-city era it is helping to usher in have, in my opinion, not been fully thought out by policymakers.

Just 200 years ago, 80 percent of the population lived in non-urban areas. Cities comprised just one-fifth of the global population. This ratio will be reversed by 2050, with 80 percent of the world's population living in mega-cities, according to some forecasts.*

This unparalleled transformation may have unforeseen consequences, as did the development of nuclear energy. In the 1950s we assumed nuclear energy would be the solution to world energy shortages. Many argued that nuclear energy was virtually limitless and brushed aside questions about the disposal of nuclear waste as a challenge future innovations would easily cope with. Since Chernobyl, however, we can no longer regard safety as a non-issue. That disaster revealed again that unreflective faith in progress can blind us to ennormous risks.

Governments continue to bend over backwards to provide incentives for metropolitan growth and centralization, arguing that this sparks economic expansion and higher national incomes. Even governments in small provinces

---

* In 1950 there were two mega-cities in the western hemisphere: New York City, with a population of 12 million, and London with 8.7 million people. By 1995 there were 22 mega-cities, with 16 in developing countries. Currently, the five largest are Tokyo (26.8 million people), Sao Paulo (16.4 million), New York (16.3 million), Mexico City (15.5 million) and Mumbai (15.1 billion). According to forecasts by the United Nations, there will be 33 mega-cities (defined as having a population exceeding 8 million people) by 2015, with 27 in developing countries.

in Canada, like Nova Scotia, have jumped on the bandwagon by encouraging the concentration of industry and universities in the capital city of Halifax.

Provincial policymakers have said they hope to lay a foundation for the burst of innovation and economic growth that occurred in the Boston-Cambridge area where the concentration of scientific resources created an environment of hi-tech and medical innovation that spurred private sector growth. (After three decades of attempting to duplicate this model, some policymakers appear to be unswayed by their lack of success.)

What happened in the Boston-Cambridge area may be inapplicable on a global scale. The concentration of people and resources in Mexico City, for example, has made the air often unbreathable, while the city's primary water source is about 150 kilometers away. Mega-cities are creating immense strains on the environment, while hyper migration in the developing world is making slums more massive and encouraging social isolation.

Moreover, we are seeing the emergence of the "global consumer" whose tastes and choices appear to be dictated by the marketplace. Whether one visits Seoul, Rio, New York or Montreal, music, fashion, automobiles and fast-food outlets are increasingly looking the same. The much touted diversity of city life may mask an emerging global conformity that crosses all lines, except economic ones. Allegiance to brand names may be replacing individuality.

Declining employment in resource-based economies is one of the causes of migration to larger and larger cities. Metropolitan centers have in turn increased their technocratic and political power, while small towns and rural areas have become both economically and socially depleted. The gap between the center and the periphery, between metropolitan areas and those outside them, is widening.

What makes this alarming to many is that traditional cultures often flourish in non-metropolitan areas. Residents of cities are more likely to conform to global patterns dictated by the market. Philosopher Bernard Stiegler has been a vocal opponent of what he has called the "hyper-industrialization of culture." He has expressed concern that people are being severed from genuine cultural experiences, and alarm that the technical ability to digitalize images and sounds may see local cultural products becoming reproduced for the global market by corporations.

Rural areas and small towns have proven to be fertile ground for the creation of authentic cultural products and events, which can create a sense of shared identity that goes far deeper than the shared experience of a global brand.

⮂ The Development Spectrum

I see world societies on a spectrum of development. Simply put, at one end there are aboriginal societies who live very close to nature and have not developed the modern mechanisms that most of us take for granted. At the other end are the post-industrial societies based on technocratic principles. What are often seen as "primitive societies" from the technocratic perspective are more highly dependent on nature (i.e. rainfall) and their members often have low levels of formal education.

Traditions, personal relationships, connection to physical places and relationship to a stable, enduring community are vital for most people. Such values, which most people cherish, have little chance of surviving in the dominant technocratic culture.

The relationship between individuals and nature in post-industrial societies, on the other hand, is mediated by technical and institutional structures intended, among other things, to provide a scheduled delivery of goods and services to meet everyday needs.

The first I call "naturalistic" and the other "technocratic." The former is rooted in one geographic place, where traditional culture, kinship and personal relationships dominate. "Who you are" is more important than "what you can do." Technocratic societies, however, are highly mobile with multiple connections to the world rather than to one place. In them, technical ability and relationship to artificial institutions dominate. What you can do is more important than who you are. Technocratic societies usually develop in large metropolitan areas, which become centers of power and wealth. Naturalistic societies tend to be dispersed. Obviously, both societies have positive and negative traits and most lie somewhere between the two ends of the spectrum.

It appears, however, that most of the world is becoming increasingly dominated by the technocratic pull. Smaller, traditional societies around the globe are being depleted and undermined by the ongoing centralization of life.

In the technocratic global system people are forced to adapt to the economy rather than the other way around. If a particular society has a very different set of traditions and deep-rooted values, then that society will simply be excluded from advancement in the system. In a sense, the world economy is like a global sport. If members of one society do not know the rules or refuse to accept them, they will be confined to the sidelines.

One personal example of this came from my experience of attempting to advise a native Canadian on the development of his lobster business. He was an experienced fisherman whose catch was usually plentiful. He should have been making a hefty profit but was not. He explained that often when he was transporting his daily catch from the boat to the wholesaler, he would run into an uncle and share some lobsters with him, then he passed his grandmother's house and would give some to her, and if a friend was sick he would drop more off at his friend's house, and so on. The point is that the culture of solidarity and sharing he lived in prevented him from playing by the rules of the profit-oriented game.

This case is a caricature, but it highlights an important point: a single global economic "game" is developing and those who do not adhere to its rules will be marginalized and suffer. Around the globe, aboriginal peoples are on the extreme end of the development spectrum, and they are paying the highest penalties. Government policies, in the past, have been to assist, or speed up, their assimilation. These polices have failed.

Some may say that aboriginal societies comprise a small minority of the world's population so to focus on them is to distort the global reality. However, I believe that most people are faced with the same dilemma, though not to such an extreme degree. Traditions, personal relationships, connection to physical places and relationship to a stable, enduring community are vital for most people. Such values, which most people cherish, have little chance of surviving in the dominant technocratic culture. There is nothing wrong with people migrating from place to place. We have a long history of doing this, but what is new is the degree of migration. "Degree" is an important ecological word: too much or too little can be detrimental.

The difference between communities where the majority of residents have lived in the same place for three or four generations is deep when compared with places where most residents were born elsewhere. Connection to place certainly has an impact on an individual's sense of history and culture. In the typical, emerging mega-cities, most residents were born elsewhere. For many, this is irrelevant; for others it is a profoundly alienating experience.

Ecologists know that the pace and degree of change is of great significance in building a sustainable future. We must be cautious when we orchestrate changes that create a new form of society and a new type of individual. In our global consumer society, a new kind of person may be evolving: one who lacks connection to a specific environment and whose identity is wrapped up in labels and products. We remain in the dark about the emerging social consequences of the this new form of human being who seems to live at the mercy of marketing campaigns.

From an ecological point of view, population concentration has dangerous side-effects. These are well known and too lengthy to list. Besides the environmental damage caused by population centralization, there are tremendous social costs, and these have ecological dimensions also. Working class families often cannot afford a home in a metropolitan center so they must live in high-rise apartments, which can make it more difficult to create a healthy social atmosphere for raising children. Schools are usually much larger and more difficult to control. Furthermore, highly urbanized areas are characterized by anonymity. Many adults prefer that, but there is a price. The social controls operational in small towns don't function in the impersonal metropolis and as a result crime, for example, poses a greater danger.

Concentration of population brings short-term economic benefits, but the long-term costs on the environment as well as social stress on families and individuals, are rarely factored in to policymakers' decisions.

⊃ The organic paradigm

Most economists use a mathematical paradigm to interpret reality. "If you can't measure it, you can't manage it," is the mantra of those who run the world's massive management systems. Dr. Marie Elisabeth Chassagne, an economic geographer who worked in policy and planning for the French government, claims that this paradigm is inappropriate for economic planning. She proposes an organic approach. In the mechanistic paradigm it is assumed that a French corporation can transfer a stove factory from Paris to South Africa just as a car can be shipped. Planners, however, are often surprised when the factory does not work as well in its new location. Dr. Chassagne argues that their mistake is embedded in their paradigm.

> After the fall of communism, immense quantities of capital were invested in Russia. We now know that the system could not absorb it and failure manifested itself in many forms.

The switch to an organic paradigm changes the analysis. Within the organic domain we know that a tree that flourishes in Paris may well die in Southern Africa. Moisture, temperature and soil conditions are critical elements for its growth and survival. If we view factories and economic organizations as organic then we must look at what economists call "the externals." We will look at the local social and political reality to determine whether it offers sufficient stability and support. In the organic world, a single tree is vulnerable, but a hundred trees will supply mutual support. Similarly, single industries parachuted into an underdeveloped nation are usually vulnerable. Different kinds of plants require different timeframes for growth and development.

Economists tend to forget that time and rate of growth can be critical for business also. The organic paradigm can be helpful in the management of capital. Too much or too little water can kill a plant. Judgment and knowledge of the organism and environment are necessary to arrive at a correct assessment. After the fall of the Soviet Union, immense quantities of capital were invested in Russia. We now know that the system could not absorb it and failure manifested itself in many forms. Too little capital or too much can kill a business.

My arguments in favour of small towns and rural communities are not based on opposition to cities. Rather, my concern is balance and equilibrium. Many cities are, in fact, organized as a collection of villages, especially in the older core areas. If smaller communities are sacrificed for mega-cities, then both will suffer. Size itself brings unanticipated problems, as discussed earlier. In a healthy country and in a healthy world that is ecologically balanced, there will be both.

It is remarkable how the culture and wisdom of ancient Greece lives on in so much of our language. Words like "architecture," "ecology" and "economics" are all derived from Greek, and a number of writers have pointed out the utility of reflecting on their original meanings. The word *oikos* or "eco" means "household," so "ecology" means understanding of the household, and "economics" means management of the household. The relationship between ecology and economics is embedded in the original meanings of the two words.

Another Greek-based word, "architecture," also comes in handy. The arch is the bridge or connector between two walls. If we think of an architect as a bridge builder, or one who connects the different parts of a structure, it becomes clear that we are in great need of architects who can help us connect the many rooms in the global household. My hope is that some readers of this book will join the movement to revitalize local communities, while keeping in mind the global trends that affect us all.

International Cooperative Alliance

> Voluntary and open membership
> Democratic member control (not controlled by capital)
> Member economic participation (members control)
> Autonomy and independence
> Education, training and information
> Cooperation among co-ops
> Concern for community

Japan Workers' Co-operative Union

> To create good jobs for citizens
> Co-management by all members
> Conducive to community development
> To be independent, cooperative and humanistic (human development)
> To maintain autonomy with national solidarity
> To establish a cooperative and not-for-profit sector
> Promote global and human solidarity

Mondragon

> Open admission
> Democratic organization
> Sovereignty of labour
> Instrumental character of capital
> Self-management
> Pay solidarity
> Group cooperation
> Social transformation
> Universal nature
> Education

Plunkett Foundation

> A community enterprise is a business which aims to create sustainable jobs and related training opportunities for local people and/or to provide commercial services.

> A community enterprise aims to make profits and to become financially self-supporting; to use profits only for investment in its enterprises, for limited bonus payments to workers, and for community benefit.

> Membership or share-holding in the community enterprise is organized on democratic one-person-one-vote principles.

> A community enterprise must be registered either as a company or as a cooperative society using a model or other legal structure which is recognized as acceptable.

> The assets of the community enterprise are owned on behalf of the community and are held in trust by the directors such that the assets may not be disposed of to benefit financially individual members or directors.

> The membership of the community enterprise must be open to all persons within its agreed area of benefit. In some circumstances a "community of interest" or a "community of need" can be established.

> The community enterprise is committed to being a good employer regarding wage levels, terms and conditions, equal opportunities and employee participation.

> The community enterprise is committed to evaluating and reporting annually on the effectiveness of its impact on the local community.

Berle, Adolfe A. and Means, Gardiner C. 1932 [1967]. *The Modern Corporation and Private Property*. New York: MacMillan

Craig, John G. 1993. *The Nature of Cooperation*. Montreal: Black Rose Books.

Davis, John P. 1905. *Corporations: A Study of the Origin and Development of Great Business Combinations and their Relation to the Authority of the State*, Volumes I and II. New York: Burt Franklin.

Dobbin, Murray. 1998. *The Myth of the Good Corporate Citizen: Democracy under the rule of big business*. Toronto: Stoddard.

Drucker, Peter. 1993. *Post Capitalist Society*. New York: Harper Business.

Friedman, Milton. 1980. *Free to Choose*. New York: Harcourt Brace.

Gower, L.C.B. 1969. *The Principles of Modern Company Law*. London: Stevens and Sons.

Korten, David C. 2001. *When Corporations Rule the World [2nd edition]*. West Hartford, Connecticut: Kumarian Press.

Habermas, Jurgen. 1985. *The Theory of Communicative Action: Beacon Press*

Helliwell, John. 2001. *Guest Editor, Special Issue on Social Capital. ISUMA: Canadian Journal of Policy Research (Spring) (www.isuma.net/v02n01/index_e. shtml)*.

Laidlaw, Alex. 1971. *The Man from Margaree: Moses Coady*. Toronto: McClelland Stewart.

MacIntyre, Gertrude. 1998, *Perspectives on Communities: A Community Economic Roundtable: CBU Press*.

MacLeod, Greg. 1985. *New Age Business*. Ottawa: Canadian Council on Social Development.

MacLeod, Greg. 1997. *From Mondragon to America*. Sydney, Nova Scotia: University College of Cape Breton Press.

Melnyk, George. 1985. *The Search for Community: From Utopia to a Cooperative Society.* Montreal: Black Rose Books.

Piore, Michael, and Sabel, Charles. 1984. *The Second Industrial Divide: Possibilities for Prosperity.* New York: Basic Books.

Putnam, Robert D. 2000. *Bowling Alone: The Collapse and Revival of American Community.* New York: Simon and Schuster.

Quarter, Jack. 1993. *Canada's Social Economy.* Toronto: Lorimer.

Quarter, Jack. 2000. *Beyond the Bottom Line: Socially Innovative Business Owners.* Westport, Connecticut: Quorum Books.

Reich, Robert B. 1992. *The Work of Nations.* New York: Vintage Books

Scott, Mark C. 2000. *Re-inspiring the Corporation: The seven seminal paths to corporate greatness.* New York: John Wiley and Sons.

Sen, Amartya. 1999. "Democracy as a Universal Value." *Journal of Democracy 10* (3): 3-17. (http://muse.jhu.edu/demo/jod/10.3sen.html)

Soros, George. 1997. "The Capitalist Threat." *Atlantic Monthly 297* (2): 45-58. (www.theatlantic.com/issues/97feb/capital/capital.html)

Stiegler, Bernard. 1999. "Mass Culture." *Le Monde Diplomatique, Supplement sur l'Avenir 2000-2009.* December.

Stiglitz, Joseph. 2001. "Thanks for Nothing." *The Atlantic Monthly (3):* 36-40. (www.theatlantic.com/issues/2001/10/stiglitz.html)

Thurow, Lester. 1996. *The Future of Capitalism: How today's economic forces shape tomorrow's world.* New York: W. Morrow and Company.

Went, Robert. 2000. *Globalization: Neo-liberal Challenge, Radical Response (Translated by Peter Drucker).* London: Pluto Press.

Also see: www.mondragon.mcc.es & www.ced.ca